Adam's L.A.W.
Lessons Along the Way

Adam's L.A.W.
Lessons Along the Way

Keep Pressing On!

Adam Harris

Additional Book by Adam Harris:

A Heart to Give: *A Journal of Transformation*
Copyright 2010

Adam's L.A.W.
Lessons Along the Way

Keep Pressing On!

ISBN: 0692416722
ISBN 13: 9780692416723
Library of Congress Control Number: 2015905365
Adam Harris, Detroit, MI

Dedication

This book is dedicated to the readers and leaders of our future. Always remember that everything you need on your journey of life has already been placed on the inside of you. Journey on in faith, knowing that hard work is required. Take one step at a time. Keep pressing on!

Acknowledgements

I would like to take a moment to acknowledge a few people in my life for seeing this project through.

First and foremost, I am blessed and honored to have my Lord and Savior, Jesus Christ in my life. Everything that happens that is beautifully and wonderfully made comes from Him. I am truly thankful for God's mercy and grace.

Secondly, I would like to thank my family and friends who encourage me to be all that God has called me to be. I am sure that naming off individual names would cause me to leave someone out, so I will take the time to thank each person individually. However, I must say thank you to my Mom, Sylvia Harris for all that she means to me in this life. I love you very much.

Lastly, I would like to thank my editors: Dr. Gloria House and Drake Phifer. I appreciate the both of you for taking the time to read my book, and challenging me on becoming a great writer. I truly love you both and I appreciate your encouragement throughout the entire process.

God bless all of you in your future endeavors with an abundance of love and life.

Table of Contents

"We are not human beings having a spiritual experience. We are spiritual beings having a human experience."

— Pierre Teilhard de Chardin

Introduction

I consider it an honor that you have chosen to read my second book about lessons that I have learned along my journey of life. Whether you know me personally, have heard me speaking at a workshop or seminar, or someone suggested that you consider purchasing this book, for your personal growth, I am truly honored. Within the pages of this book you will find personal life lessons that have empowered me.

Over the years, I have been blessed with the opportunity to encourage, inspire and mentor many young people. I would like to continue providing such inspiration and encouragement. Countless people have placed nutritious fruit and vegetables of information in my personal basket, and through my life of service, I want to share what I have received with you. I take heed of the African concept, *UBUNTU which means "I am because we are, and we are because I am."* It would not be possible for me to write this book without the great teachers, mentors and friends that I have in my life. More importantly, these individuals challenge me daily to live up to my purpose in this earth.

Please know that this book is Volume One of the lessons that I have learned. I will share with you many more lessons in the future. In each chapter, I have presented a life lesson that will evolve over time as you revisit it from time to time. One thing that I enjoy most about the human experience is that growth and development is a life-long process. As you continue to live your life, the lessons that I have shared with you will have different meanings as the years pass.

Throughout the book, I explain how I have been personally impacted by the lessons that I am sharing with you. I chose to personalize the lessons because I wanted to illustrate that I am still learning and in the process of becoming what I feel my life was created for. Each lesson also carries quotes that I have been inspired by, and words of wisdom from people contemporary and historical, who have impacted my life.

So again, I say how grateful I am for your purchase of this book, and for allowing me to share with you lessons that I have learned along the way. I hope that you find value, encouragement, hope, inspiration, challenge, faith, love and restoration within the pages of this book. May God bless you in all of your future endeavors. I look forward to being empowered and inspired by you in the future - *Reciprocity*.

Open a Book

By Amber
5th Grade Student, Detroit

Open a book
And you will find,
People and places of every kind.

Open a book
And you can be,
Anything you want to be.

Open a book
And you can share,
Wondrous words you find there.

Open a book
And I will too,
You read to me and I'll read to you.

I Am

Dear Future Leader,

Has anyone ever told you how beautiful you are? Has anyone ever said that you are unique and one of a kind? No one who has lived before you, and no one who will live after you will ever be made from the blueprint that you were created from. You are simply one of a kind. An original.

I hope you take moments in your life to ponder and reflect on what makes you who you are. Discover the gifts and talents you have. Notice the things that make you smile, the things that make you laugh, and the things that make you sad. Discover those things that you are passionate about. What do you hope to accomplish in the future? What are some things that you know you can improve on? This work is only for you to do because no one knows you better than you.

As you begin to discover just who you are, remember that you will continue to grow as life moves on. Take time to reflect during different stages in your life, and during times of adversity and calm. This will allow you to discover the inner resources you have, and how you can engineer a better you for the future.

Just remember that there will never be another YOU! Live your life to the fullest.

With Agape Love,
AH

"You were born to be different because you were made to make a difference."

— ADAM HARRIS

I Am

"The greatness of this period was that
we straightened our backs up. And a man
can't ride your back unless it's bent."

— Rev. Dr. Martin Luther King, Jr.

One of the greatest lessons in life that you can understand and comprehend is knowing who you are. And when confronted with the question, Who are you?, it's not good enough to provide the name you've been given at birth, what race or culture you identify with or what you've been called; but more important is understanding what makes you unique, and recognizing the gifts and talents you bring to the table that tells the world, *"I am me, and there will be no one else like me."*

Over the past few years, I have had the privilege to facilitate workshops and presentations with young people in K-12, at the college and university level, and in the community, posing the question: **Who are you?** And in order for me to ask them that very question, I had to look in the mirror at myself, and ask the same question. I was reminded of the lyrics of a song by Michael Jackson:

"I'm starting with the man in the mirror. I asking him to change his ways." Asking myself this question, caused me to dig deep into the crevices of my own life and soul to understand why I am who I am. For example, I took the time to list the values that I carry, considered the qualities and attributes that I try to portray and live by, and reflect on the experiences that I have had up to this point in my life. This work provided context and insight into why I am compassionate, kind-hearted, forgiving, spiritually rooted, etc. Everything that we experience in life, whether good or bad has an effect on who we are. These experiences can even provide insight into why we feel confident, complacent, easy going, strong mind-ed, nervous or even fearful as we approach opportunities (e.g. relationships, job opportunities, future goals, dreams, aspirations, conquering fear).

One day I was a part of a group experience for a high school event that was working to foster a school climate of understanding, acceptance and respect amongst the students. The school flew in professionally trained facilitators from California to facilitate a large group experience that took place between more than a hundred students in the school. During one of the discussions, one of the facilitators mentioned that people are like icebergs; the part you can see is only a small percentage of the bigger picture. **However, the part of the iceberg that you cannot see, the part that exists below the surface is truly who we are as individuals.**

As I began to take time to think about the concept of the iceberg, I realized how much sense it really made. So often we only see the physical frame and body image that was given to a person by birth. We observe these tangible items of a person through our sense of sight and touch, and we begin to make assumptions through our socially constructed realities. Then through our own world views on life, we classify individuals and attach certain preconceived notions to certain people.

However, what is even more interesting is when the person is unsure of who they are, and they accept and internalize these constructed ideas and notions of what others think. From there the person begins to believe what others think about them, and then they start to internalize the new reality as a part of who they really are. Eventually this belief becomes a self-fulfilling prophecy, where the individual starts to act and behave on this newly constructed belief.

Too often I see young men and women who give away power to a person with whom they are in conflict. During these moments, one person plays the victim and expresses that their behavior was dictated by the unkind words, actions or behavior of the other person. The victim places sole responsibility outside of themselves, and feels that the situation was caused, perpetuated and evolved to the extent that it did because of the other person.

The value of knowing who you are empowers you to take responsibility for yourself and the things that you can control. One of my favorite quotes by Reinhold Niebuhr says, **"Lord, grant me the serenity to accept the things I cannot change; courage to change the things I can; and wisdom to know the difference."** You may not be able to control the things that happen in your life, for example: deaths, illnesses, circumstances, the way people feel about you, events in your life, people's actions toward you or even experiences that you may go through. However, you do have control over your actions, your behaviors, your responses, how you feel about yourself and others. This power that you have is beneath the surface of your image and is knitted in the fiber and essence of your being. You can discover these inner resources by looking beneath the surface. *When you place blame on someone else for your actions and behaviors, you have displaced your own power and established that you are a **puppet** to the external forces of life. This question might sound silly; however* **are you a puppet???**

Dr. Martin Luther King, Jr. once said: ***"The greatness of this period was that we straightened our backs up. And a man can't ride your back unless it's bent."*** Through my days working as a staff member in many schools, I would recite this line by Dr. King to students who said they were being picked on or bullied. I am certainly aware of the fact that bullying is an issue that our society must take seriously, as it has a long-lasting impact on those affected by it. However, over the years, I have taken time to consider the role of the victim and the fact that it requires that a person give away some of their own power in order for another individual to have control over how they feel about themselves. Now for kids, bullying can be a more complex issue. It is important for them to feel safe, and know that there are people who love them, affirm them and care for them so that how they see themselves is reinforced by those who believe in them. When children live in this environment of love, the hope is that they will grow into adults who are strong and capable of facing the harsh realities of society. When their upbringing is rooted in the soil of support, encouragement, love, good values, beliefs and morals, they are able to stand firm when the winds of hatred blow.

My lesson to you in this chapter is to really do the work to know who you are. Take time to look below the surface of your iceberg to discover what makes you the only "You" that will ever exist on this earth. **No one who lived before you, and no one who will live after you will ever be blessed with the basket of gifts and talents that you are created with.** When you finally discover and understand the true you, *e.g. good, bad, culture, history, life experiences, family, dreams, goals, fears, qualities, attributes, etc.*, that make up the knitted fibers that make you who you are, no one can ever tell you otherwise because you know that you are the one to write the story of your own book. **You are the sole author of your story and only you hold the pen.**

So be very careful how you write the story of your life. Also pay attention to those you give credit to in your story. Don't give your time or attention to those who don't believe in you, betray you, hate you, or reject you. Give credit to your faith, your resilience, your dedication, your persistence, being steadfast and unwavering in your pursuit of your goals. Recognize that each passing moment allows you to write new entries and chapters to your story, and in those moments you will realize that you can be creative to write the story as you see it to be. For myself, I have discovered that **I am a servant. I am**

a survivor. I am a leader. I am a helper. I am an edu-
cator. I am a dreamer. I am an author. I am a thinker.
I am a man. One thing is for certain, if you are not yet
who you want to be, *today is your moment to start being
who you know you can be.* Look beneath your surface to
discover who you are, so that you can begin working on
what you are called to be.

Who Are You?

Dear God,

I take this moment to say thank you for creating me just the way I am. I know that when I consider my life through my eyes, I am only considering what I can see. At times, I have only concerned myself with my image and what others can see about me. Lord, teach me to see me as you see me. Take me from the limited scope of my view point to observe my life beneath the surface where I am able to discover truly who I am. The real me.

You have blessed me with many gifts and talents that I will continue to discover throughout my life. I know that I have only begun to scratch the surface of the iceberg of seeing truly how you made me and more importantly what you've placed on the inside of me. Continue to reveal the greatness that exists inside me, and let that greatness make its way on the outside so that your glory can be revealed in the earth. I love you and thank you for this temple you've created. I will align my will with the path you have created for me.

With love and thanks for all you've done and all that you're going to do in my life and through my life.

In Jesus Name,
Amen!

Service

Dear Future Leader,

I wrote this chapter specifically for you. During my journey at the University of Michigan in Dearborn, I didn't really discover what made me unique until I began being of service to others. Through many opportunities, I learned about my innate and unique abilities to be of service to others. I realized I enjoyed listening; I enjoyed helping people move from one place in their lives to the next; and I looked forward to challenging people to be the very best they are capable of becoming. These are the reasons I went to graduate school to earn a counseling degree.

I hope that you can discover your unique talents and gifts, and work on becoming your best. No one on this earth is anything like you, and you were created and designed for a specific purpose in this life. Be your best. Accept and expect nothing less!

With Agape Love!
AH

"When you give, you live. However, don't just live your life. Have L.I.F.E. while living. Live In Faith Everyday!"

— ADAM HARRIS

Service

"Service is the rent we pay for the privilege of living on this earth."

— *Shirley Chisholm*

One of the purest opportunities in life is the gift of service. Whether your time is spent volunteering at a local shelter, passing out food for the holidays, building a ramp for someone who is disabled or spending time to read to children, these moments are priceless. We can never place a real dollar figure on what our service means in the lives of those we serve. However, the truth is that some of our greatest champions and world leaders discovered their path in life through service.

During my days as an undergraduate student at University of Michigan-Dearborn, I committed to memory a quote by Mahatma Gandhi: **"The best way to find yourself is to lose yourself in the service of others."** My mind was perplexed in trying to understand how I could find myself by becoming lost. Today, I have a better understanding of the meaning of this statement, and how service to others can help individuals discover their way in life.

In the first chapter of this book, I explained that one of the greatest lessons in life is understanding and knowing who you are. I mentioned how essential it is for you to look beneath the surface of your own iceberg to understand what makes you unique, while realizing that there was and never will be another person on this earth like you. One of the ways that you can discover the treasure that exists below the surface is through opportunities of service.

Through my experiences in life that involved providing a service to others, I learned a great deal about our society, the human experience and myself. Through each experience, I looked forward to giving of my time and being of assistance to others. Surprisingly, each time I walked away, I felt that I had learned more about myself than I ever knew I would.

Growing up as a child, my family and I would serve on a daily basis at our storefront church in the heart of Detroit. There would be times when I would question my father as a young kid, asking, "Dad, why are we helping these people whom we know nothing about?" My Dad would simply respond, "Son, we have been blessed beyond your imagination, and regardless of how bad you may feel we have it, someone else always has it worst." It was years later before I would finally grasp what my dad was saying to me, and understand the value of service in the lives of others. **I now understand that service rendered to others is service to oneself.**

My days at the University of Michigan-Dearborn served me well. Not just because I received a great education and a degree from one of the most prestigious universities in the world, but more so because I was putting my education from the classroom into practice. I notice that the mission of many educational institutions states, "Enter here...and go forth to serve." As for my university, service was a key component to the university's belief in making a Metropolitan Impact. The Chancellor of the campus believes that education should go beyond the classroom, and should engage students in project-based learning experiences within the community. For me, the idea of education being an applied learning experience had already been made clear throughout my early childhood.

In my first book, entitled *A Heart to Give*, I wrote about my experience of service in the Gulf Coast region, in efforts to rebuild communities devastated by Hurricanes Katrina and Rita that made landfall in the early 2000's. I took time to chronicle my thoughts during my experience. During my time of service to the region of Southwest Louisiana, I thought that my efforts (along with those of other college students) would help to make a meaningful impact in transforming lives and the local communities there. We certainly made a difference in the lives of local families, agencies in need and individuals who needed assistance getting back on their feet. **What I didn't realize was how my engagement would have an even greater significance in transforming my own life and helping me to discover my passion and purpose in life.** I was a different person upon returning to Detroit. I even gave up playing college basketball – a game that I loved very much - to immerse myself in community service for my entire senior year.

Service provided me the opportunity to discover my abilities to help others reach their goals in life, to move individuals from point A to point B. It allowed me to discover that in moments of despair, I longed to be someone's hope; in moments of difficulty, I longed to ease someone's burden; in moments of transition, I longed to just be present. It was through service and moments of volunteering my time in Louisiana that I found what my next educational journey would consist of: a master's degree in Counseling. Simply put: I long to ease the transition process for people by empowering them as they move from one place in their lives to the next.

So my lesson in this chapter is to help you realize the unlimited value and distinct privilege inherent in the gift of being of service to others. As I read through the annals of history, some of the world's most recognized icons and greatest heroines were servants. If you look at Mahatma Gandhi, Mother Theresa, Dr. Martin Luther King, Jr., Nelson Mandela, Susan B. Anthony and even our 44th President, Barack Obama, their lives were lost in the opportunity of service, and their paths were discovered because of it.

As you move forward in life, remember that one avenue to discover the great treasure that exists on the inside of you is through service. It allows you to look below the surface of your iceberg, and see the gifts and talents that you have. You will also be able to tap into just how great you really are, and the great things you can achieve on this earth. As Dr. Martin Luther King, Jr. pointed out, "Everybody can be great. Because everybody can serve." **I challenge you to discover who you are through service because you were created to do great things.**

"Do all the good you can, by all the means you can, in all the ways you can, at all the times you can, to all the people you can, for as long as ever you can."

— *JOHN WESLEY*

What have you discovered about yourself through service?

Dear God,

Thank you for giving me my hands because you remind me that they are useful for lending a hand. Thank you for giving me my feet because you remind me that I can go into places where my help is needed. Lord thank you for giving me my eyes to see because I can notice when tears fall, when someone is hurt, when someone is sad, when someone is homeless, when and where you can use me. I realize that I do not need a degree to be of service, but as one of your great servants once said, "You only need a heart full of grace and a soul generated by love." (Dr. Martin Luther King, Jr.)

Lord, thank you for the opportunity to be of service to others. When I give of myself, I am reminded of your son's journey to purely give of himself while expecting nothing in return. He provided humanity with a great example of laying down one's life for our brothers and sisters that we may share this journey of life together.

Lord, teach me to find you in the midst of service, and reveal to me aspects of who I am while I serve others. As I look to bless others through my acts of benevolence and generosity, let your light shine brightly so that others can find you in those moments. You are the Mighty One, Prince of Peace, Morning Light, One Who Rescues, Light of the World, Balm in Gilead, Source of Hope, True Bread from

Heaven and True Place of Rest. Show up in my time of service.

With a heart to serve you and a life to love you. I will live for you.

In Jesus Name,
Amen.

Moments Serving My Community

Congratulating high school seniors for making a
decision to pursue college after high school.
Plymouth Educational Center. (Detroit, MI)

**Presenting to students at University High School
for Black History Month** *(Ferndale, MI).*

**Presenting to high school students at Westside Christian
Academy for Black History Month** *(Redford, MI).*

Visiting WDIV Channel 4 with high school students from a metro
Detroit mentoring program, Building a Focused Future (BFF).

Group photo with young men in college at the
national SAAB Conference *(Dearborn, MI)*.

With children in Rio de Janeiro, Brazil (2010).

Keep Pressing On!

Dear Future Leader,

The forecast ahead is cloudy, with storms coming in at 90 miles per hour. I forewarn you so that you may realize that it is time to strap up and consider what is heading your way. What I am sharing with you is not meant to scare you. I am simply preparing you for the journey ahead.

If I can be truthful and honest with you, the journey up the mountain is not easy because each step you take will move you higher into the atmosphere. You will notice that as you climb, many will be heading back down the mountain because they were not fit for the climb. Whether due to a lack of physical fitness, emotional stability, mental preparation, spiritual maturity or confusion concerning why they started the climb, many will start the journey but few will finish.

There will be many sacrifices along the way. The time it takes to prepare alone will cause you to miss significant events in your life. If you don't learn to say no, you will begin to lose focus on what's in front of you. As you lose sight of that which is in front of you, you will begin to lose your grip and footing, and your ability to make the best decision for the next step up. There will be an onslaught of distractions to take your eyes off the prize. It will be up to you to stay committed and determined to let nothing stop you.

So when times seem rough and the going gets tough, just remember to keep pressing on. Remember that everything you need is already inside of you, and your biggest challenger will be you. It was Robert Browning who said, "Ah, but a man's reach should exceed his grasp, or what's a Heaven for." I encourage you today to keep going.
Keep Pressing On!

With Agape Love,
AH

"Learn to take the hate with the weight. Just make sure to keep your back straight. Let your haters be your motivators, your escalators and your elevators. Their energy should be used to move you to the next destination in your life."

— ADAM HARRIS

Keep Pressing On!

"When you are going through something,
don't stop."

As the Christmas and New Year holiday season came around during the month of December 2005, my Mom gave me a holiday season's greeting card. On the inside of the card, she simply wrote, **"Keep pressing on!"** To this day, I'm not sure if my Mom knows how much those three words meant to me and still mean to me today. Those three words were my saving grace during a time when I was seriously thinking about quitting school. At that time in my life, I had just finished the fall semester of my sophomore year at the University of Michigan-Dearborn. I remember being at a lull in my academic experience, and I questioned whether or not I wanted to persist with college. I was considering dropping out of school and I was planning on doing so without discussing it with anyone. I questioned whether or not college was for me, and if I had what it took to make it through.

Now that I am almost 10 years away from that point of reference, I am certainly glad that I did not turn back.

I remember hearing about how some of my old friends were "enjoying life" and having fun by allowing high school to be the final stage of their formal education. I heard about the parties I missed, and the countless social gatherings I had to forego to truly immerse myself in my education. It was tough hearing about these things, and turning down invitation after invitation to say, "Sorry, I can't this time." **However, every missed opportunity provided me new opportunities for what I longed for in my future.**

At that time in my life, it was my first year playing basketball for the University. I had sat out my entire freshman year to establish a solid first year academically. In my second year, I started getting the hang of the new college environment, began bonding with my teammates, feeling the comfort to reach out to classmates for different assignments and projects, and I began to really embrace the idea that I was a student at the University of Michigan. And even with a solid academic year under my belt and getting comfortable with the university's system, I still felt as if I had a long way up the mountain. I could feel that I was beginning to penetrate another part of the atmosphere, where the air becomes still, and holding onto the rope of hope was of vital importance.

During this time, my classes were getting tougher than those of my freshman year. I was juggling playing basketball, working at Meijer, being a student, being a family man, and volunteering my time in my community as a youth basketball coach. Some of the classes required a more intense focus and dedication to scholarship. Many of my classes during that time were pre-requisites for my acceptance into the College of Business the following year. I had to really buckle down. I was entering a new dimension in my academic experience that had me question my ability to climb the mountain that was in front of me. I had already invested a year in my education on the way up, but at the same time, I was looking down the mountain, and considering dropping out.

I really appreciate that there are college breaks throughout the course of an academic year. A break was exactly what I needed. The time off gave me the opportunity to reflect, be with my family for an extended period of time, focus on playing basketball and take a little bit of time away from my studies. The Christmas break allowed me time to rejuvenate, to reflect on the new level that I had reached academically, and to appreciate the fact that I did not quit during the semester. Lastly, it provided my Mom a moment and opportunity to hand me a Season's Greeting card that imparted three words that I desperately needed for motivation, **"Keep pressing on!"**

When I was working on my internship for my master's degree, my supervisor once said to me, *"When you are going through something, keep going. Don't stop!"* During my internship experience, I established a close bond with my boss that it allowed me to be open and honest about the trials that I was facing at the time. There were days that I came to work questioning whether my service to students was making an impact or whether I should continue encouraging others to stay committed on their journey, while I felt like quitting myself. My finances had gotten so tight that I had lost my car for a period of time, and I was behind in rent for my apartment. In the midst of my despair, my boss's words were the calm in the middle of my storm.

Early on in my life, I remembered learning about martial arts. I used to love watching martial artists who demonstrated that people have the ability to punch through cinder blocks. One thing that always stood out to me was the mental drive, fortitude and commitment required in a split second to strike through all the cinder blocks. I remember learning that if you eased up during that split moment, you could be badly injured. Hesitation could lead to a broken arm, a shoulder out of socket or a crushed hand. I learned that it was of vital importance to focus all of your attention and effort to the task of punching through all the blocks. I share this analogy of not letting up if you seem to be punching through your own cinder blocks in life because adversity and hard times will meet up with you on your journey. When you face those challenges, you will need to keep your focus and not let up or get distracted as you punch through the cinder blocks in your life.

On your journey, you will face moments where you will want to turn back and head down the mountain. You will feel tired and weary at times and even consider easing up in the pursuit of your goals. You may even believe that you are losing the battle of time, and maybe you should reconsider the requests of friends to remain comfortable. Well, real champions understand that it takes courage to keep going, mental fortitude to keep pressing onward, and when the times seem bleak, commitment to keep moving forward. **During the challenging times,**

I remind myself why I started in the first place, and it provides the emergency generation of power that I need to finish what I started.

So my lesson in this chapter is for you to keep moving forward on your journey ahead. At times you will question whether the pursuit of what you are after is worth it. Much of this struggle is human nature and the mental battle we face daily to reach beyond what we have already captured. It was Robert Browning who said, "A man's reach should exceed his grasp." Some people tend to settle on past victories and accomplishments, and become idle in the comfort of complacency. On your journey of life, you will face distractions, moments where you feel that the load is too heavy, times when you will question your ability, and moments when you will doubt and consider going back down the mountain. But all of that is nothing but **F.E.A.R.** (False Evidence Appearing Real), and you can either choose to *Forget Everything and Run* or *Face Everything and Rise*. I hope that you choose the latter.

While you are in the midst of your press, expect the best and accept nothing less.

Please know that your journey will have some haters and some cheerleaders on the sidelines; however, never forget that you are the one in the game and each play you make influences the final outcome. Just remember that you did not make it this far because of luck or coincidences. You are alive and here today because your journey has purpose, and the tasks in front of you need your commitment, drive and mental fortitude to be completed. **You**

must believe that this is your time to keep pressing onward, and just know that anything worth having is worth fighting for.

I learned this lesson from my Mom and I am forever grateful for her belief in me and for her pushing me forward during a time of weakness. I love you Mom. I will Keep Pressing On!

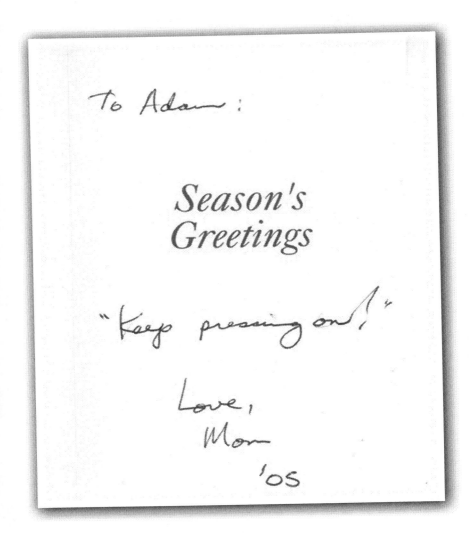

To Adam:

*Season's
Greetings*

"Keep pressing on!"

Love,
Mom
'05

Dear God,

I enter your presence with thanksgiving and unwavering love because your love is unconditional. When I least expect it, your mercy saves me in times of danger and your grace carries me in times of weakness. Lord, I notice that you know when times are tough for me and when adversity seems to strike on every side. You have encamped your angels all around me to keep me safe and protected.

Father, as I look back over my life, and I consider where you brought me from, I have no other words to say other than THANK YOU for everything you've done in my life. You seem to know when my well is getting dry, and when I need water to quench my thirst. You seem to know when my spirit is running low and you sweep in a new found joy and everlasting peace to rejuvenate me. You notice me Heavenly Father when my physical being is tired, and you create space for me to rest. So I again say thank you for all that you've done, all that you're doing and what you're about to do.

Lord, when times are rough, help me to keep pressing on. When times are good, Lord, elevate me to another level in giving and living for you. Father, when I can't see my way and the path in front of me, cast away fear so that I trust you and keep pressing onward. When I feel broken, and everything around me tells me to quit, give me the endurance to run this race for you. I know that when you are in it, there is no limit to what can be accomplished and achieved.

Heavenly Father, I put my trust and belief in you to guide me the rest of my days. Keep me pressing onward and toward the mark of the high calling. I can feel you suspending me from your mighty wings of love and I ask that you continue carrying me into my destiny.

I love you and give your name the praises for all that you've done.

In Jesus's Mighty Name,
Amen

Dream BIG!

Dear Future Leader,

One of the greatest gifts you have as a human being is the ability to dream. With this gift, you can imagine things that have never been, and use what you've envisioned to create things that have never existed. This gift gave a young preacher from Atlanta, Georgia the ability to communicate his vision to America on the Lincoln Memorial steps in Washington, D.C. in 1963 (Dr. Martin Luther King, Jr.). This gift provided Henry Ford the idea to put the world on wheels with the automobile. This same gift gave the Wright Brothers the vision that people could travel faster in the air inside the molded pieces of metal that we now call airplanes.

Use the gift to dream wisely, and know that you can use it to change the trajectory of your life and the lives of others in the future. You are a leader and you can also be a dreamer. Dream Big.

With Agape Love,
AH

Dream BIG

"We must never stop dreaming. Dreams
provide nourishment for the soul, just as a
meal does for the body."

— *Paulo Coelho*

Every great invention, idea, success or manmade cre-
ation started with a dream. Whether you consider the
automobile, the traffic light, the air plane, cell phones
or computers, they all began with a dream. It is important that you first understand that you have the ability
to dream, for those who follow their dreams, journey
through life as if their lives are a part of a different time
zone. They realize that time is of the essence. Dreams
are just like seeds that you plant; the soil, the environment, sunlight, rain and nourishment are all vital during
the growing process. Be very careful where you scatter
the seeds of your dreams.

Some people dream of having a life where their family
can prosper. They search for safe neighborhoods, good
schools, and clean and quiet places to rest their heads at
night. For another person, a dream may be more of the

day to day grind of making ends meet, and enjoying the presence of loved ones who bring joy and excitement to each day. For someone else, a dream may be looking to beat the odds and striving to be the first in their family to accomplish a big task, such as going off to college and graduating. Maybe your dream involves landing a corporate or salaried job, or possibly being an entrepreneur and starting your own business. Whatever the dream is, it should provide hope and vision for each day, so that your daily tasks sprout from the seeds you plant. The seeds that are planted should be saplings of hope for what's to come in the future.

The Greek philosopher, Aristotle, said, ***"Hope is a waking dream."***

Ambitious dreams provide vision to your life. Amazingly, through dreams we are able to catch glimpses of our life's potential and possibilities from the viewpoint of an eagle. Dreams take us above the valleys, over the hills, and through the mountains to see where our lives could end up if we commit ourselves to our journey in life. It's as if we are back in our childhood days, looking at the movie, "Aladdin," and taking a magic carpet ride above the world to reach that place we dream about.

One thing that I must warn you not to not do is get caught up in the web of your dreams. Often I talk to people at different stages of their lives who have amazing dreams, ideas, and visions for their future. When the time comes to actualize their dream or come down from the eagle's viewpoint to work in the field to make it happen, many get scared and turn back because they didn't process how tough the terrain and journey would be to fulfill their dream. I always remind myself of a quote by Paul Valery: *"The best way to make your dreams come true is to wake up."*

Most people know at least one person who has a dream in life. However, when you ask the person, "How is your dream coming along?" there often times seems to be an excuse that precedes taking ownership of their reality. They are not ready for the challenge.

For some people the excuse that precedes their taking ownership of the challenge can be:

- Fear of the unknown.
- Fear of added pressure and responsibility that comes with living out your dream.
- Fear of failure or things not turning out the way you envisioned.
- Fear of unfinished business that may come back to haunt you.
- Fear of not having what it takes to sustain yourself for the journey.
- Fear of your own potential, and how others may perceive you while you are on your way to your destiny.

There is a long list of fears, excuses and reasons that I might have mentioned, but I will give you space to write your own. Take a moment to think about what's holding you back from living out your dreams, and manifesting the God-given abilities and talents that you have. I want you to write them down. After you write them down, I want you to gather up the courage to look them in the eye.

Fears, Excuses & Setbacks...

Fear that I'm not good enough.
the way I am
Fear that I will give my all
and still come up short.

Now that you have faced your fears, take a moment to say bye to each one. Let today be the last day that they stop you from reaching your destiny or living up to your God given abilities. Feel free to say out loud:

"As of this moment, I will not allow any of you to hold me back from reaching my destiny. As of this moment, I will begin to walk in my purpose and live out my dreams. I will turn my face from you and claim in this earth what I know is mine. This will be the last conversation that I will have with you because you've been in my life too long."

One thing that I am certain of is that it takes courage and strength to look inward and say, "I am the one I have been waiting for." Mahatma Gandhi said, *"Be the change you wish to see in the world."* This is a very simple concept, but again it takes courage and strength to do. How long will you allow yourself to make an excuse for not going back to college to get your degree? How long will you allow others to believe that you are chasing after your dreams, when you know that you are like the woman at the well **(John 4)**?

Or simply put, how long will it take you to stop settling for less, when the rest of you wants to become the best you?
(i.e. relationship, career, lifestyle, personal, family or financial).
The TRUTH is...It's up to you!

I would not be able to write about this without having learned it through experiences in my own life. As I was finishing my senior year of undergrad at University of Michigan-Dearborn, I began working on my first book, *A Heart to Give,* which I wanted to publish. During the summer of 2008, I completed my manuscript and I was all prepared to consider publishers to make it happen. When the time came to start considering avenues I could take to make my dream a reality, I started making excuses and reading over the book to see if I wanted to add more or if I wanted to make further changes. The reality was I was dealing with FEAR. I did not have the courage and strength to acknowledge my fears, look them in the face and speak life over my situation.

I began to wonder how others would perceive me as a young author. I thought about releasing my ideas, making them available to the public, and I knew that once released, they were copyrighted in the Library of Congress, and if I wanted to change something, there was no turning back. I also considered explaining why I had written the book, my purpose in publishing it. At the end of the day, I battled with FEAR, and it took me two long years before I finally published my book in 2010.

I quote my good friend and brother in this journey of life, Dr. Eddie Connor, Jr. who says, "Your test will be a testimony. Your misery will be ministry. Your mess will be a message." This was very true for me back in 2010, and it is still very relevant in my life today.

My hope is that you will begin to dream bigger than ever before, and after you have established your dream, I hope you begin working to make it a reality.

Dr. W.E.B Dubois said, *"It is a hard thing to live haunted by the ghost of an untrue dream."* Every day is an opportunity for you to work toward making your dreams come true, rather than dreaming life away. It's okay to take moments to envision life from the viewpoint of the eagle or through the vantage point of Aladdin on the magic carpet; however, make sure you toil the fields and valleys of life to make your dreams come true. **Don't shy away from grabbing hold of your life and doing the necessary work to make things happen. Please understand that _everything you need is already with you and in you_.** You are the person you have been waiting for, so DREAM BIG and then wake up and make it happen.

Dear God,

Teach me how to dream beyond the limits of my imagination. You are the creator of what has been and what's to come. Only you know the capacity of my capabilities, and I want to see the reality of your purpose revealed in my life. I know that when you created me, you wanted me to dream. I am reminded of this when I lay my head to rest, and you allow me to journey to places that I have never been before.

Today I ask you to stretch me. Show me who I am through your eyes, and more importantly where you see me through the plans you have for me. You are the architect, the potter and the captain of my ship. I trust and believe in you. Teach me to DREAM BIG!

Your humble servant.
In Jesus Name,
Amen!

Hope

June 15, 2014 - 4:16pm

From the distant shore,
It is because of you that I still believe.
Even though the times seem bleak,
I keep pressing for I am destined to succeed.

Each day feels different.
Some days are clouded with gloom;
But every day that I rise with breadth in my body,
I know my daybreak is coming soon.

I know that if I keep you at the core,
My faith will carry me through.
Continue to be the pulse of my life,
Because my goals, dreams and hopes all depend on you.

So until my last days come,
I will ride you like a ship upon the sea.
You will be my comfort, my strength and my confidant,
Until I fulfill what God has called me to be.

Victory and Defeat

Dear Future Leader,

I am excited that you have made it this far through the book. It says a lot about you and your eagerness to continue learning and growing. I hope that up to this point in the book, you have broadened your perspective on life, while picking up nuggets of information that can help you along the way. I am truly excited for all that you will accomplish in the future.

In this chapter, I wanted to bring to the forefront the understanding that you will experience both victories and defeats along the way. When we experience the victories, we feel as though all our hard work paid off. Victory is a testament to our persistence, dedication, commitment and blue collar mentality. However, when we lose in battle, we tend to discard all that the journey has taught us. We forget about the experiences (whether good or bad) that we had, the individuals who committed to the journey with us, and the personal and mental growth that we gained through the process.

At this point in your life, I hope that you know that losing in battle does not mean that you are a loser. Learn how to reframe the experiences that you go through so that you have insight concerning how you can change things for the better in the future. Hopefully you can consider the broader scope of things and see that the race that you are running is not a sprint, it is a marathon. Make sure that you humble yourself in the times of victory, and be gracious in times of defeat. I wish you all the best on the journey ahead!

With Agape Love,
AH

"You have no clue what God is going to pull you through, neither what God is going to take you through. However, what's more important is where He is about to take you to."

— ADAM HARRIS

Victory and Defeat

"Be humble in victory and gracious
in defeat."

During my junior year at University of Michigan in Dearborn, I remember sitting in the lockeroom after a conference basketball game that was on the road. After being destroyed by our opponent and feeling humiliated by a horrible loss, I remember our assistant coach addressing the team with thoughts and comments about the game. There was a quote that he used to address our team that I have chosen to carry with me for the rest of my life. He simply said, **"Be humble in victory and gracious in defeat."**

Along your journey of life, it is unrealistic to think that every battle that you fight will be a victorious outcome in your favor. I know that winning 100% of the time would be ideal, but realistically we need losses to remind us of our weaknesses and areas where we can improve.

As a coach for high school girls' basketball over the last several years, I have seen countless teams win in their division and be undefeated throughout the regular season. However, when the state playoffs came around, there would be a shocking story that would make the headlines in local newspapers. The undefeated, highly ranked team in the state of Michigan was knocked out of the playoffs by a team that everyone expected the undefeated powerhouse to dominate. The story would shock sports reporters who had made their predictions in favor of the undefeated team. Now the headline would read something along the lines of "David knocks down Goliath."

Taking a loss graciously can sometimes be the best thing that can happen to you and for you. At some point in your life, you may find something that you are extremely good at. Matter of fact, you may be so good at it that you will be able to do it effortlessly and still be better than most who are trying to compete against you. **When you discover that gift you have that allows you to perform effortlessly and still be considered the best, you have possibly found a God-given treasure that was uniquely designed just for you - *Your Talent.***

A few years ago, I was blessed to reconnect with my middle school band teacher, Randy Scott, an international jazz recording artist. What I found to be so amazing about my former teacher was his God-given talent to play the saxophone. He has played with many great musicians from all around the world. In all of his performances, he leaves the crowd in awe of his gift and musicianship. On another note, what's so amazing about his character is the humility he shows as his gift inspires people to come alive through music.

In some of my conversations with Randy over the years, he has shared with me that he makes sure to listen to other saxophone players that he considers to be great or musicians who have a skill on an instrument that he would like to develop. He explained to me that though he is conscious of his gift, he is always looking for ways to get better. He listens to all genres of music and he even takes lessons from other professional musicians to improve his skills. It was during those conversations that I realized how great a musician he really is.

When you can acknowledge others in your field who are great at what they do, and recognize your own areas for growth, you will find value in your gift and discover the worth of investing in the talent you have. It takes maturity to reach a point in your life to be grateful for the gifts you have, while at the same time recognizing the gifts and talents in others.

When Thomas Edison was experimenting with the light bulb, he went through many trials and errors (losses) to finally find the effective solution. When he was questioned about his experimentation, he said, **"I have not failed. I've just found 10,000 ways that won't work."** What's so amazing about his journey to provide electrical light for our world is that he did not quit after the first loss, the second, the third...etc. He continued to experiment because he knew that each trial that concluded in an error meant that he was one step closer to true victory. He proved that the process of elimination was a valid method of finding the answer to a problem.

Michael Jordan, who is arguably one of the greatest basketball players of all time, said, **"I have failed over** and over and over again in my life, and that is why I succeed." Frequently in his career, Jordan was trusted to take the last shot in close game situations, with everyone hoping that he could make something miraculous happen. He would do all that he could to prepare himself for those moments when they came. He was the hardest working player in the league, and he put the time in the gym, taking thousands of shots a day. His will to win was unquestionable. However, he always understood that there were always two options that could play out with any shot – either he would make it or miss it. The key to his success for the moments that he has been praised for was his ability to block out everything around him except the shot clock, the rim and his ability to take his best shot. Everything else that followed was okay for him because he knew he had prepared himself, whether the outcome turned out positive or negative. He understood that a make would give him praise; however, a miss would only drive him to improve and get better.

So my hope in explaining this lesson in life is to remind you that whatever your competition or challenge in life may be, know that you will fail at times along your journey of success. Please remember that failing at a task does not mean that you are a failure or that your life is over. Pick yourself up, dust yourself off, and keep it moving. Once you realize that failing at different tasks along the way is a part of the territory of reaching the pinnacle of success in your life, you will become wiser and more in tune with the journey in front of you. Every trial and error will make you better, and every defeat and loss will make you stronger and more equipped for what's ahead.

For each shot you take, you will develop better precision and accuracy. In every victory and defeat, you will gain more experience that will remind you that you've faced difficulties before. The test in front of you will be easier this time around. You will pass with flying colors, all because you were prepared through victories and defeats. At that moment in your life, you will move to a new level of self-confidence.

You have what it takes to be successful, so don't give up or give in to the wins and losses along the way. Be the best. Except and expect nothing less. You were made to withstand the tests. Believe in yourself because you are closer to achievement than you think.

"I've missed more than 9000 shots in my career. I've lost almost 300 games. 26 times, I've been trusted to take the game winning shot and missed. I've failed over and over and over again in my life. And that is why I succeed."

— *MICHAEL JORDAN*

Dear God,

I enter your presence today in awe of your power. With all that is going on around me, you find a way to penetrate the noise of everything that surrounds me to give me a word from you that always blesses me and reminds me of your grace, your mercy and your favor in my life. I am grateful for your open line of communication, and I appreciate you for listening to me and speaking to my spirit.

Father, in this moment I want to express gratitude for battles that I experience along life's path. I know that with every battle, I may experience victory or defeat based on social circumstances; however, I am more thankful that each trial neither makes nor breaks me. I also know that with you, I am always a VICTOR. I have learned that some experiences take longer to conquer than others, but there is one thing that I know for sure: You are victorious in everything I go through because nothing can destroy you.

So, precious Father, keep me in the mighty wonder of your power, and remind me of the gift of resilience that I have inside me. I am more than a conqueror through your son Jesus, and He has already paid the cost for all of my pain and suffering.

God, I love you, thank you, glorify you and bless your holy name. You are a mighty wonder and an amazing God. Thank you for being present every day of my life, and I look forward to all that you will do in my life and through my life.

In victory, I am reminded to be humble. In defeat, I will be gracious.

In Jesus name,
Amen

Pain

June 8, 2014 - 12:30am

During this journey of life,
I promise you will feel pain.
For each experience is different,
And neither one will feel the same.

At times you may want to quit,
At times you may want to turn to your past.
In these times remind yourself why you started,
Because each step gets you closer to your destiny at last.

There will be moments where the pain will wear on you,
You will notice your eyes constantly observing the ground.
During these times I remind you to hold your head up high and
stand
Because around the corner your victory trumpet is ready to
sound.

So keep the faith and don't give up
Because pain is an ingredient of God's plan.
You see, if pain didn't exist or you never had rain,
How would you ever get stronger and turn your pain into your gain.

You will make it, this I promise
Because trouble won't last always.
Each day you wake up, should serve as a reminder
That your latter days will be your brighter days.

So good tidings for the journey ahead,
And to all the challenges you'll face.
Just remember to never give up on God
Because He will help you run your race.

S.T.A.N.D.

Dear Future Leader,

I am sure by now that you understand that being a leader is not an easy task. Matter of fact, it is a heavy responsibility. The territory of leadership itself brings pressure. You have people who look to you for guidance and direction, and those who consider you to have special gifts. The truth is the role that you play has ups and downs, so it can be a blessing and burden at the same time.

The message in this chapter is to strengthen you to STAND on your beliefs and values, even if you have to stand alone. Throughout your life you will grow physically, spiritually, and intellectually. During this growth process, you will have moments in which your values, morals and worldview will be confronted and challenged. The more you learn and the more mature you become, it is possible that you may adopt new perspectives and ideas on life. Don't be afraid of these changes because they indicate that you are growing. At the same time, don't allow fear to cripple you so that you hesitate to do what's right when the decision is not popular among those you lead.

Dr. Martin Luther King, Jr. said, **"The time is always right to do what is right."** In your role as a leader, make sure that you S.T.A.N.D - *Stand Tall And Not Divided* on what you believe is right when it's your time to make decisions. Have your feet rooted in good soil, and have the confidence to step up to the plate and deliver. Be willing to accept the consequences and potential backlash if it comes because you know that you did the right thing.

I will be praying for you, and hopefully you can do the same for me.

With Agape Love,
AH

S.T.A.N.D.

STAND TALL AND NOT DIVIDED
Loyalty - *"Be true to yourself. Be true to those you lead."*

— *JOHN WOODEN*

In an earlier chapter in this book, I wrote about the importance of knowing who you are. When you have an understanding of who you are, the added value that you realize is higher self-esteem and self-worth. Knowing who you are brings self-affirmation and a way of saying to the world, **"This is who I am, and I STAND on what I believe."** Other by-products of knowing who you are include mental fortitude, individual strength, esteemed pride and having the courage to *S.T.A.N.D* during the tests and trials in your life.

When I was in elementary school, I committed to memory a saying that still plays a foundational role in my life today. Malcolm X said, **"If you don't stand for something, you will fall for anything."** The older I get, I see the significance of this adage and why it serves a purpose in my life today.

When you are growing up, your parents teach you morals and values that uphold your lifestyle - the way you look at the world, things you should and should not do, and ways you should handle conflict and other situations. As you get older, you are exposed to different experiences and opportunities that will allow you to stand firm on those beliefs and values or alter and change them as you see the need to do so.

It was through my college experience that I truly discovered what I stood for and believed. I also learned about the things that I questioned or was still unsure about. In our ever changing society, we are constantly exposed to new ideas concerning diversity and inclusion. This is not surprising when you consider that we can access information and meet people from across the world through modern technology. We can learn about issues and cultures of foreign countries, create relationships with individuals using the internet, and have conversations about how the decisions of one country may impact the entire world. I remember leaving many conversations with friends, colleagues and people that I met along the way, asking myself, who am I, what do I believe **and what do I S.T.A.N.D for?**

I've learned so much from people through intellectual, social, cultural, and religious conversations, and I discovered questions that I had never even asked before. Some of the conversations left me pondering a new way of looking at the world, and considering adopting a new value or life lesson.

Everyone has a values system and worldview which informs their beliefs, perspectives, thoughts, and feelings toward others and society as a whole. When I began to process this, I realized that it was important for me to be open minded, but also rooted in knowing myself and **STAND**ing on what I believe so that I could add value to the world in my own special way.

As a leader, you will face diverse people, ideas, values, beliefs, and thoughts concerning the best ways to lead those who follow you. You will be pulled in many directions when you consider your personal, public, and professional life. In these moments, you will find a great deal of value in knowing who you are, knowing how to align yourself with opportunities that fit your passion and purpose in life, and most importantly, knowing the importance of **STAND**ing on what you believe.

John Wooden, who led the UCLA Bruins to 11 National Championships over his years as the head coach of the Men's Basketball team, said, **"Be true to yourself. Be true to those you lead."** He considered loyalty as a foundational principle in his *Pyramid of Success*, and he believed that you must be true to yourself and to those you lead. If you expect others to be loyal to your leadership and follow you in the terrains of your vision, it would be in your best interest to know who you are and have a solid idea of where you are headed. An old cliché' says, **"If the blind leads the blind, they will all fall in a ditch."**

I hope you take time throughout your life to consider the values and beliefs that matter to you. As you travel through life, no one except the Creator will know you better than yourself. Be confident in yourself, and be true to who you are and what you believe. As you establish the foundation and core of who you are, you will notice that things around you will align with your passion or purpose or they will be like the leaves on the trees in the fall season - they will blow away with the wind.

The world is waiting for you to be the true you, and your involvement is needed in local communities throughout the world. Be willing to STAND on what you believe and the foundation of who you are. Know that you will be a better leader for it.

Be true. Be you. There will never be another you. Stand Tall And Never Doubt.

Dear God,

I come into your presence at this moment with my head bowed, but my spirit lifted, because you have the power to make me whole when I feel broken. I want to take a moment to just say thank you for life, health and strength because those alone are blessings that you continue to give me each day. I am honored to call you my friend, for I know that you are the only one that I can truly count on who will never turn your back on me. And for that I thank you and give you praise.

At this moment, I simply ask you to give me the strength to STAND when I need the courage to face difficult decisions. Even though I may be ridiculed, chastised, rejected and disliked for the decisions that I will have to make, in these moments remind me of your son's journey and how he was the foundation stone that the builders rejected.

Give me the power to believe. Give me the faith I need to achieve. Give me knowledge and wisdom to succeed. I cannot do this alone. I need you every step of the way. Guide me, teach me and assist me along the way, for it is toward the hills I look for my help. I know my help comes from you.

I love you and will continue to praise you as I STAND.

In Jesus name,
Amen

Forgive

Dear Future Leader,

Have you ever gotten yourself ready for a vacation? You took the time to pack everything that you needed to have your best outfits, the shoes that matched each outfit, and you packed all the body wash, lotion, and fragrances that you needed for the trip. When you arrived at the airport to check your luggage, you were asked to condense what you had packed because your bags were overweight. Well, this chapter is all about examining what you are carrying in your luggage and letting go of the past hurt and pain that you don't need to carry on your flight to your destination of success.

So often we think of only one aspect of the act of forgiveness, as a pardon for someone else's wrongdoing. We forget that this benevolent and compassionate act was also created for the liberation and restoration of our own soul. It is all about freedom for you, letting go of the old so that you can open up your hand to receive things that are new.

Whatever you are carrying that is not enhancing your life, I pray that you subtract that from your life, and forgive whoever or whatever the situation or circumstance was. In an earlier chapter, I encouraged you to Keep Pressing On. I explained that you are on a journey up the mountain, looking to reach the pinnacle of success. On that journey, you do not need to carry extra luggage because the steep slopes will wear you down and you will be exhausted before you can complete the journey.

When you withhold forgiveness from those who have caused you pain, you leave open doors that should have been closed. The doors that you leave open are back alley ways for bitterness, pain and hurt to return from your past. Get rid of the things from your past so that you can live in your purpose at last. If you would like to ascend to the next level in your life, there must be closure on the past. FORGIVE. LET IT GO.

Apostle Paul said, "Brethren, I count not myself to have apprehended: but this one thing I do, forgetting those things which are behind, and reaching forth unto those things which are before..." (Philippians 3:13). It is your time to rise, but you must also realize that everyone and everything cannot go with you. Leave behind the old and prepare for the newness of life that is in front of you.

Be blessed with a life to live through your compassion to forgive!

With Agape Love,
AH.

"Don't let your past days be your last days. If you are going to die in a box, why live your life in one? The fact that you are living means you still have purpose. You're redeemed, so live your dreams. You're restored, so claim your reward. You're never rejected nor neglected, just redirected and reconnected."

— ADAM HARRIS

Forgive

Let it Go!

"The most noble cause known to man
is the liberation of the human mind
and spirit."

— DR. MAYA ANGELOU

One of the greatest lessons that you can ever learn is the lesson of forgiveness. Jesus teaches us this lesson when he mentions how we should pray. The Lord's Prayer says, "And forgive us our sins; for we also forgive everyone that is indebted to us." (Luke 11:4). If we go further into the life of our brother Jesus, his very last words before transcending the boundary of this earth were: "Father, forgive them; for they know not what they do." What a blessing it is to know that the son of man who was 100% human and 100% divine took a stand for those who nailed him to the cross. When he could have turned his back on us and allowed God's judgment to bring resolve to this world, He loved us so much that He endured the test so that we could be blessed. "For God so loved the world that He gave his only begotten son." (John 3:16).

Even though forgiveness is one of the greatest lessons you can ever learn as human being, it can also be one of the most difficult lessons. How can you forgive someone who hates you, degrades you and looks down upon you? What about forgiving someone who rejected you? Or what about someone who mistreats you or inflicts pain and evil upon you? The truth is people often believe that when they forgive others, they are letting a person get away with a wrong that they believe should be brought to justice. Our mind processes the act of forgiveness as letting the wrongdoer get away. In fact, it is just the opposite. Forgiveness is for the wounded, the hurt, those in pain, and those who have been betrayed.

Forgiveness pardons those who have sinned because the Bible explains that we were born into sin and shaped in iniquity. However, forgiveness allows the wounded and those hurting to experience freedom and liberty. True forgiveness prevents those who have done wrong to us from holding us hostage in the prison of spiritual captivity. Their intention is to take captive the mind, and make you feel embarrassed, trapped, rejected, isolated, depressed, lonely and forgotten.

One of the worse feelings to experience is walking into a room and not knowing that a person who once caused you pain, discomfort, and distress is in the same room with you. When you notice that the person is present, you often feel past wounds open up that you thought were healed. You thought that you were able to move on from the past; however, in that moment you are reminded that you have unfinished business that you did not take care of. It could have been that you never faced the person to say how you really felt and tell them that they would no longer take up mental space in your life. Maybe the person or situation reminded you of a past childhood experience in which you did not have the courage to stand up for yourself, and you felt helpless and weak. Or maybe it was an experience or relationship where you were totally invested – you gave everything you had to the relationship (i.e. money, time, care, loyalty, commitment, physical, emotional and spiritual etc.) and you were left with nothing in return. What is so intriguing about the adversity that we face is Jesus understands these experiences. He gave up his throne to experience life on this earth in the flesh to teach us that we can persevere and keep pressing forward.

A scripture from the Bible, in the book of Matthew, 18th chapter, verses 6th and 7th, reads:

6 But whoso shall offend one of these little ones which believe in me, it were better for him that a millstone were hanged about his neck, and that he were drowned in the depth of the sea.

7 Woe unto the world because of offences! For it must needs be that offences come; but woe to that man by whom the offence cometh!

In this chapter of Matthew, the disciples are having a heated discussion where they ask Jesus, "Who will be the greatest in the kingdom of heaven?" Jesus answered that it is important that we humble ourselves like children.

In his response, Jesus is not encouraging to be child-ish, but rather childlike. If you think about the nature of children, you see that they are sincere and genuine as to their feelings, their ambition to dream and their hon-esty of thought. It is through their eyes and world view that as adults, we can be reminded of life's simple lessons and the things that truly matter. Somewhere along our journey of life, we get older and lose sight of these simple lessons, and it is our children who can reset the fuse box to the life lessons we already know.

In the same discussion that the disciples were hav-ing about who will be the greatest in the kingdom, Jesus mentions that offending a child would bring conse-quences: "But woe to that man by whom the offence co-meth." He says that it would be better for him to have a millstone hung around his neck, and be drowned in the depth of the sea. This is why it is so important to value and respect the lives of others. In God's eyes, we are all considered His children. The wrong that we do know-ingly and unknowingly can have an impact on the emo-tional, mental and psychological well-being of a person. Our negative behaviors can leave mental scars, emotion-al wounds, psychological despair and tombstones on the ambitious dreams, hopes and goals of others.

At the beginning of this chapter, I mentioned that the Lord's Prayer says, "And forgive us our sins; for we also forgive everyone that is indebted to us." Whenever I recite this prayer, I am reminded that I am not per-fect, and that I am in need of God's forgiveness to move forward under the protection of His grace and mercy. Through the same lens, I understand that others will make mistakes, and the mercy and grace that I need is the same loving kindness that God extends to all His children.

So in reality, forgiveness is not about justice having its due process, it is about making sure that we free ourselves from the mental bondage, past hurt and pain we have gone through. Forgiveness creates space for healing to take place. Forgiveness says, I will not allow this person or situation to have control over my feelings, my thoughts or my conscious any more. Forgiveness creates a place for us to say, "May God have mercy on their souls." It says, "God, I have turned this problem over to you and because I know that you know what happened. I leave it up to you to balance the equation."

Forgiveness is a process, and for each person it can take time to manifest itself and take root. However, my hope is that this process takes root in you so that you can liberate your mind, body, soul and spirit. You should know that God loves you, and He is waiting to restore your ultimate joy and peace in this life. What is so interesting to me about the story of Jesus, and His lesson of forgiveness that I love so much is He showed us that in order for us to rise, we must forgive and lay down the burdens of those who have done us wrong. Jesus wanted to be liberated from the sins of this world, so he said, **"Father, forgive them...."** I can only imagine that it must have been a lonely experience on that day at Calvary for our brother Jesus because no one spoke up for him. After all the people he healed, fed, delivered, pardoned, brought back to life and counseled, He was put to death without anyone taking the witness stand on His behalf.

My hope is that you allow yourself to lay to rest the past (i.e. embarrassment, pain others have caused you, and disappointment in yourself for bad choices) and cut the rope tied to the millstone on your neck. Learn from the things you have gone through, and don't allow yourself to repeat those experiences. You are deserving of the same blood that Jesus shed on Calvary for this world, and He wants to be your friend in this journey of life. Forgive those who have done you wrong, and forgive yourself so that you can be at rest and peace in your life. When you forgive, God can take you to higher heights.

Dear God,

At this moment I come into your presence humble and grateful for your loving kindness. At this time I recognize that it is because of you that I have breath in my body, and more importantly I have a life to live. Father, I am thankful for the life of your son, Jesus, who died on Calvary's cross for the sins of this world. It is because of the blood He shed on that day that I have saving grace.

Father, I need you to teach me the lesson of forgiveness. This valuable lesson was expressed greatly and lived out beautifully through the life of your Son, as He taught us how to ascend to another level of living. His very last words were expressed to you on the cross when he said, "Father, forgive them for they know not what they do." Lord, teach me the lesson that your son lived, even if I feel that the whole world is against me. I know that with you on my side, there is more power with you than all those who are against me.

Teach me to pardon others when they cause me pain and distress. Remind me that the grace and mercy that I need is the same that I should give out to others. I know that if you can forgive me for my sins, then I can forgive others for their wrongdoings.

I take this time to acknowledge your presence, your power and favor as the Foundation Stone and the beginning and the end. I give my heart, with a life to live and a time to forgive.

In Jesus Name!
Amen

Activate Your Faith

Dear Future Leader,

As you read this chapter on Activating Your Faith, I simply want you to know that no dream is possible without your persistent effort and diligent work. It is so easy to get caught up in your creative imaginations (i.e. dreams) that you can forget that if you don't go into labor, you can never give birth to your dreams. Going into labor is the process of putting your dreams into action, and doing whatever is necessary to give your dream a pulse of life.

I love to refer to a saying by Thomas Edison: **"What it boils down to is one percent inspiration and ninety-nine percent perspiration."** Edison is saying that in realizing a dream, the inspiration, the original idea, counts only one percent, while work, the 99% is what is necessary. There are many people who are waiting for a miracle or for someone to give them the keys to their ideal future. The truth of the matter is the only way you will get there is taking one step at a time, one day at a time, and believing every step of the way that you will continue working to give birth to your dreams.

So now, all eyes are on you. What you do from this point forward will speak to your credibility, your word, and what you stand for. Are you willing to go the extra mile? Are you willing to make sacrifices that will help you stay focused on your journey and the destination ahead? Are you willing to put in the necessary work to make your dreams a reality? Newsflash: No one will do it for you; however, if they do, please know they will take all the credit for investing in your amazing dream.

This is your moment in time to shine. Don't let your dream be carried away by the ocean's current of fear. You can do it. You will do it. Make it happen.

With Agape Love,
AH

"Don't live your life in vain. Run in your own lane."

— ADAM HARRIS

Activate Your Faith

"Keep your dreams alive. Understand to
achieve anything requires faith and belief
in yourself, vision, hard work, determination, and dedication. Remember all things
are possible for those who believe."

— *GAIL DEVERS*

If you are determined to get anywhere in life, you must
be willing to invest time into your own work. This means
that you descend from the clouds of your dreams, put
your hands to the plow, and get the work done. You get
stronger after each repetition, and you become savvier
in your strategy of making things happen. It can be very
easy to speak about the things that you long to achieve,
but nothing is more significant or important than the
work you put toward your goals, dreams and ambitions.

What I truly love about this phase of the process is you
begin to learn who is a true foot soldier with you on your
journey. You will meet many people along your journey
who will say they are with you, and that they have your
back. However, I dare you to start putting your hands to

the plow, and then take a look to the right and left of you to see just how many people will be standing with you. I can promise you that those who said that they believed in you the most, may be the ones who blow away like the wind. It could be that they were in your life during those times for a reason or a season, but not for the long haul.

"One is not born in the world to do everything, but to do something."

— HENRY DAVID THOREAU

At times I am amazed by the dreams and aspirations that people have shared with me. There are people whom I have met who have dreams that can literally change the world. We have all have been given unique gifts and talents that were customized to fit every situation and circumstance that we go through, from childhood to adulthood.

One day I was on a phone conference with committed men around the state of Michigan, who are invested in their local communities and seeking ways to make a difference through mentoring. A very close friend of mine who was moderating the discussion shared a story that I want to share with you. The title of the story is **"Everybody, Somebody, Anybody and Nobody."**

This is a story about four people named Everybody, Somebody, Anybody, and Nobody. There was an important job to be done and Everybody was asked to do it. Everybody was sure Somebody would do it. Anybody could have done it, but Nobody did it. Somebody got angry about that, because it was Everybody's job. Everybody thought Anybody could do it but Nobody realized that Everybody wouldn't do it. It ended up that Everybody blamed Somebody when Nobody did what Anybody could have done.

As I have taken the time to think about life and the many gifts and talents that God gives to each person, I am sure that one of the richest places on the earth is the graveyard. I believe the graveyard is symbolic to the many dreams that have died a premature death. There are dreams that were conceived in the minds of people and carried in the souls of many; however, those dreams were never realized because there were only a few individuals who were courageous enough to risk putting their hands to the plow and activating their faith.

In the Bible there is a parable about talents that were given to three servants by their master, who was about to leave on a journey. One servant was given five talents, another servant was given two and the other was given one talent. The parable states that their master entrusted his servants with his talents, but the servants understood that he would return. The man who was given five talents went and traded with his talents and gained five additional talents. The servant who was given two talents was able to trade his talents and gain two more talents. However, the man who was given one talent went and dug a hole and buried his talent. When the master returned, the servants who doubled their talents were greeted with, "Well done, good and faithful servant. You have been faithful over a little; I will set you over much. Enter into the joy of your master." To the servant who hid his talent, the master was upset and said, "You wicked and slothful servant! You knew that I reap where I have not sown and gather where I scattered no seed? Then you ought to have invested my money with the bankers, and at my coming I should have received what was my own with interest." The master then took the one talent that he had given the servant and gave it to the servant who began with five.

There is a very important lesson that can be learned from this parable, which teaches that **we must learn how to be good stewards over what we have been given.** When I consider the message of this scripture, I wonder if the servant who was given the one talent looked at the others and asked the question, "Why was I only given one talent when the others received two and five talents?" Maybe the servant felt embarrassed, as though the master was saying that he could not handle more than the one. Or possibly the servant thought, "What can I do with just one talent?"

So often we look around us at the paths of others and we consider the gifts and talents that God has given them. We see how others are being elevated and blessed and we believe that every aspect of their journey was easy and privileged from start to finish. We even begin to compare our journey with someone else's - instead of focusing on our own. Comparing ourselves with others creates a distraction for us because as we look from side to side, we lose focus, forgetting about the hurdles, potholes, stumbling blocks and oncoming traffic we face ahead. In those moments what we fail to realize is the fact that *to whom much is given, much is required and expected.* It is not in your best interest to focus on how someone else is being blessed or to compare your life with someone else's because what God has for you is for you.

My hope is that you activate your own faith and manage the talents and gifts that God has given to you. **Regardless of the role you play in life, you were blessed to withstand your tests and to perform at your best.** Once you realize that you were designed to be an original and not a carbon copy of someone else, then you will understand that your path in life will be unique from everyone else. Your struggles will not be the same as someone else's, neither will your triumphs be the same. My only question to you is are you willing to put the work in and make things happen in your life? **Your perspiration should be much greater than your inspiration.**

As you move forward in life, I promise that you will notice people on the sidelines cheering you on. However, at the very same time, you will have those who will root against you and hope that you fail (HATERS). Those who are cheering you on, be thankful and grateful for them because some of them may become close friends, colleagues, mentors and individuals you will consider as family. However, those who are hating you or wishing for you to fail, be grateful for them also because it means you have checked into the game and you are no longer on the bench watching.

Let your haters be your motivators, your elevators and your escalators. Allow them to move you to your next destination point in your life.

Whether you believe it or not, the haters are good for you and they serve a purpose on your journey. They are there to bring balance to your life and to keep you grounded. Think of it this way: for every time you are hated, it is just as if someone were throwing dirt on you. However, the last time I checked, seeds not only need water, sun, and oxygen to live; **seeds also need DIRT as soil to grow**. The deeper the seed is in the ground, the better the chances are for the roots to grow firm and the plant to stand strong over time. Your haters will keep you grounded and humble. They remind you that there is always more work to be done. So I say to you, be thankful and grateful for your haters.

Now it is up to you. **Make the choice to use the voice inside of you**. Put in the work, invest the time, and activate your faith. You have others in the world who are counting on you. Bring life to your dreams not only because you have the ability to do so, but be a role model to someone else so that they can bring life to their dreams. Your journey should be a living testimony to what you believe, and each day you should strive to get one step closer to your dreams. Make it happen and activate your faith.

"Do all the good you can, by all the means you can, in all the ways you can, at all the times you can, to all the people you can, for as long as ever you can."

— JOHN WESLEY

Dear God,

What an honor and privilege it is that when I call on you, you are right there waiting for me to enter your presence. You are never too busy to answer and open your loving arms to me. The very fact that you are waiting on my call tells me how much you value our relationship. For that reason alone, I take a moment to say thank you.

Father God, I ask that you give me the courage to activate my faith and the strength to endure the trials that may come my way. I call on you today because in order for me to walk into the purpose that you have for me, I know that I must get to work. Lord, you said in your word that faith without works is dead. I know that it is not enough for me to wait by the well for a miracle when everything I need is already inside me. You have equipped me with the resources and tools to make my dreams come alive.

Lord, search me and examine the vault of my heart. Whatever doesn't align with what you have destined for me, please remove it. It does me no good to store inventory in my warehouse that is outdated. Get rid of faulty thinking, any signs of disbelief and all manner of evil and ungodliness. I know that you are able to do exceedingly, abundantly above all that I can ask or think. Revive me, renew me, refresh me and create a new version of me that is ready to overcome life's obstacles. I trust in you every step of the way. I've seen you do it before in the lives of others, and I know you will do the same in my life.

So today I look to you, the Master Potter, and I ask that you keep your holy hands on my life while you mold me and make me into the vessel that you want me to be. I trust you and believe in you because your blood never loses its power. Thank you for your love and your everlasting compassion.

In Jesus name,
Amen

Today Is Your Moment!

Dear Future Leader,

Dr. Benjamin E. Mays said: "Every man and woman is born into the world to do something unique and something distinctive and if he or she does not do it, it will never be done." Today is your moment to reveal the greatness inside you. Whether you believe it or not, you were created for this moment in time. Don't let this moment pass you by without making everything of it. Walk in your purpose and show the world that you are the one that you have been waiting for. Be the best. Be you. There will never be another person like you.

With Agape Love,
AH

Today Is Your Moment!

"God gave you a gift of 86,400 seconds today. Have you used one to say thank you?"

— *William Arthur Ward*

Now that you have made it to the end of this book, it is now time for you to invest in your dreams, your life and your future. Every lesson that I have shared with you was intended to help you realize your own potential. Each moment in your life creates an opportunity for you to share your gifts with others, and each day that you are alive should remind you that your life has purpose and significance. Regardless of what you were able to accomplish in the past or whatever unfinished business you still have left to do, I hope that you use today as an opportunity to move closer to your destiny.

One thing that always amazes me is the countless number of New Year's resolutions that individuals make every year, declaring that they will make a significant change in their lifestyle, health, relationships and goals moving forward. Since I was a kid, I was never too fond of the idea of resolutions for the New Year because I always felt that each moment and each day that I was blessed to be alive was an opportunity to make a change in my life. I always said to myself, why would I continue traveling down a road that I know is not getting me closer to my destiny? When I become aware that I am not fulfilling my goals in life or when I realize the winds of resistance are trying to hold me back, I understand that it is up to me to change the direction I am heading and press forward. It is important that you know that you have to take responsibility for your life and hold yourself accountable for your own actions and the decisions you make daily.

Instead of having a reaction to every action, take a moment to discern a response to stay the course.

I recently signed up to be a mentor for a non-profit organization in Detroit called Midnight Golf. The mission of this organization is to improve under-served young adults' personal development, educational preparedness and appreciation of the game of golf. Through this program, 130 high school seniors from across metro Detroit are mentored during their senior year in preparation for college. The students are equipped with the necessary tools and life skills through mentorship to succeed during the college admissions process and beyond. The students are paired with over 40 professional mentors from the surrounding Detroit area who volunteer two evenings of their time during the week to encourage the students and give them confidence that they can achieve anything they put their mind to.

One of the most impactful experiences of the program happens during our small group conversations, known as 'Tee Time', that are facilitated by the mentors. I will never forget my first Tee Time conversation in which we were basically getting to know the students (i.e. name, school, favorites and how they heard about the program). As the conversation unfolded, we discussed with the students their motivations for joining the program, what they expected to gain from the experience, and the sacrifices they had to make to be a part of the program. As the conversation began to wrap up, I used the time in my small group to articulate my thoughts on being a new mentor in the program, and the ways I believed the students could use the game of golf as a tool to be the best person they can be in college and in life.

In my opinion, golf is the one game that requires concentrated focus and determination as you approach each shot. The game requires confidence, focusing all of your energy into each shot, and blocking out distractions that may exist around you. It also requires being prepared for the physical elements of nature (i.e. wind, rain, sun, temperature). Lastly, you must have a peaceful state of mind, so you can relax and not be thrown off by unexpected events and the bad shots you may take.

In the many encounters that I have had working with young people, I have observed that they are in constant search of self-empowerment to face the challenges on their journey to success. I have sat with youth, young adults and individuals in later parts of their lives, and I have listened to the many dreams that people have. I have listened to the hopes people have for the future, and the goals people set out to accomplish years down the road. I am always amazed at the goals and dreams that people have; however, having dreams without the willingness to put the work in turns each dream into a wish. **Life should not be a place for you to count the days that pass; spend each moment making the days count as you pass through.**

Some people pass through the years with only dreams and hopes because they are simply wishing for a miracle to happen in their life. They wait by the well for a hero to carry them to their destination of success. I believe if you don't take the opportunity to breathe life into your own dreams and hopes for the future, then they will never come to life. I remember hearing a wise man say that the richest place in the world is the graveyard because there are many people who die with their dreams inside of them.

So my question to you is, **"What is your dream worth?"** Do your goals and hopes for the future have value? If so, what are you waiting for? If you know anyone who is giving away millions of dollars to make your dreams come true without your putting in any effort or work, please let me know. Thus far in my life, I haven't met that person.

"Man cannot discover new oceans unless he has the courage to lose sight of the shore."

— *ANDRE' GIDE*

Every day you have 86,400 seconds that God grants to you to make a difference in your life, someone else's, in the community, on your job, in your education, and in the world. If God grants you this gift every day, my question is what are you giving to God in return? *Or in other words, what is your gift to God?*

Can you imagine receiving a gift of ingratitude, bitterness, unhappiness, anger, discontentment, hatred, unkindness, resentment, or alienation etc? So often we look at our situation and say to ourselves, if I only had this, I would do that. Or if I had this amount of money, I would make this happen. **Please know that you have everything you need to make your dreams come alive, and if you don't bring them into the world, my question is - who will?**

This is your moment. This is your time. Don't let another day slip away without living in your purpose, heading toward your destiny. Every piece to the puzzle you are looking for will not be handed to you. It takes your believing in yourself and trusting in the process while staying the course toward your destiny. It will all be revealed to you along the way; however, it is up to you to take the first step. Make each day in your life count, so that you don't stand by and count your days. Be blessed and make it happen. Start today. Start NOW!

Dear God,

I enter your presence at this very moment knowing that all things are possible with you. You gave me air for my body to live, and a soul for my spirit to give; I know that I am destined to bring life into this world. I am thankful because life is not limited to the beauty of a new born baby, but can manifest itself in the ability that you have given all of us - the power to call those things which are not as though they were (Romans 4:17). I know that if I can conceive it in my mind, I can achieve it with time. You have given us the power through faith to give birth to our dreams. However, you taught us that faith without works is dead (James 2:26).

Heavenly Father, as I move forward in life, give me the strength and the courage to make each day count. I want to make the best of the gifts that you have given me because it was you who saw the best in me. Let what is in me be revealed to others so that they may see your good works. It is in you that I live and have life, and I hope that the candle that burns in me ignites the flame for others.

In this moment, I step back and allow you to lead me and show me the way that you want me to go. I have learned time and time again, I cannot win without you. Be my guide, my light, my pathway to a better future in you and allow others to be connected to you through the gifts and talents you have loaned to me.

I love you. I honor you. I submit my body and will to you. I give myself to you. I honor this moment because this is the day that you have made, so let it be a moment that I bring a dream to life.

In Jesus name,
Amen

This Is Your Moment!

Inspired poem for the election of President Barack Obama

We made it through adversity, pain and fear.
Looking back, I'm surprised I ever doubted.
Those who believed, hoped and prayed for change,
Expressed emotions of joy as they shouted.

We climbed mountains, been through storms,
And lost battles along the way;
For every battle lost, we paid the cost.
There's nothing to be ashamed of, I'll say.

Endured the tough times, prayed and cried,
Believing this day would come;
Pressing forward now because our daybreak is here,
As I look up, I see the sun.

So honor this moment, for God is real.
His power exists all throughout this land.
If you ever need a reminder, be aware of your hope,
And tell yourself, **"Yes You Can"**.

Graduation Day.
Receiving my Master of Arts degree in Counseling from the University of Detroit Mercy (May 2012).

Lesson from My Father

Lesson from My Father

"Seek to save all. Look to help one."

— *ALLEN B. HARRIS*

One of my true goals in life is to live each day to the fullest so that when I look at myself in the mirror, I have no regrets. There is no heavier weight to bear in life than knowing you are created for a purpose; however, when reflecting back on the time you've spent working toward your purpose, you realize a great deal of it was wasted. Time is very precious, and no man has the power to turn back its hands. Each day brings the gift of opportunity and a moment to be grateful that we can continue pressing forward.

"Yesterday is history. Tomorrow is a mystery. Today is a gift."

— ELEANOR ROOSEVELT

This chapter is simply a moment to recognize a hero that played a critical role in the development of my life. My Dad was an amazing man. I know others may think that it is the right thing to do, to pay respect to the man who created me; however, my reason for recognizing my father is different. He showed me how to live a life that was created with purpose and for a purpose. He modeled by example.

Dear Dad,

I can't believe it has been 17 years since the last time I saw your face. There are moments when I find myself wondering where the time has gone because it seems like yesterday that you were here with me. As time moves forward, I remember the times that we had and the powerful life lessons you shared with my siblings and I to be good people, and to treat people with kindness. You not only told us to put God first in our lives, you showed us by involving us in the process. You insisted that we pray for others. We woke up every morning to read scriptures and to praise God as a family, and we were engaged in serving people in the community daily. You were a true example of the man you wanted me to be, and because your lifestyle served as a model, you left behind a blueprint and foundation on which I can stand. I promise to **STAND TALL AND NOT DIVIDED.** So I take this moment to say thank you!

As I look back on all the things you shared with me, I realize how blessed I truly was to have you as my Dad. I realize now how true the statement is that you don't know the true value of something or someone until they're gone. I miss your smile, your strength, your compassion, your teachings, your work, your love, your challenge to all of us to love one another as Christ loved us, and your courage to stand firm on your beliefs even if you were standing alone.

I now know that you knew that any day standing alone was never truly a moment alone because our God above is omnipresent and omnipotent. He was always by your side, and more importantly you allowed a space for Him to dwell in your heart, which was noticeable to those who met you.

As I look back, I realize that every day for you was a day that had purpose and intentionality. I watched you use your gift of carpentry to build an empowerment zone for people less fortunate and to assist those in need on Mack Avenue in Detroit. We documented records in the thousands of people who came from near and far to receive food for their bodies and nourishment for their souls. You prayed for people, and had us join in to pray for those who asked for prayer. I saw you give hope to the hopeless, strength to the weak, encouragement to those discouraged, and a voice to the voiceless. I saw you then as my Dad, and today I know that I was blessed to have a great man of faith in my life.

To say that I miss you, doesn't quite capture the emotional, mental, physical and psychological space that has been in my life since you have made your transition to your heavenly home. When you passed, I used to believe that if I could be half the man that you were, that I could one day be great. Reminiscing on all of the lessons you have taught me, I know that you would've

been disappointed in me to think that way because you would say, "Don't sell yourself short,
son. I was only trying to be more like Christ."

Every now and then I have flashbacks to the
last moments I saw you conscious and able to
respond to the people around you. We were at
the church on our regular tour of duty and
you were sweeping the sidewalk outside. A lady
came inside the church from outside saying,
"There is an elderly man outside who has fallen
and he is struggling to get up." Mom shouted, "Go
check on your Dad." As we rushed outside, my
heart was pumping extremely fast because in
a quick glimpse from the distance I saw you
reaching for the wall in order to get up. At
that moment I didn't know what was going on
because I was only twelve years old and I had
never seen you that weak.

When the doctor at the hospital reported
to us that you had a stroke and an aneurysm, I
remember seeing you lose strength on one side
of your body. As my older brother and another
man from the community helped to get you into
the van, I remember praying for you, and holding your strong hand. In that moment, I could no
longer solely depend on the faith, prayers and
belief that you told me about. I now had to call
upon God Almighty myself. This time it was real.
With tears streaming down my face, I asked
God to heal you, and I told you over and over, "I
love you Dad."

In the days that have passed without your physical presence, I have graduated from middle school, high school, University of Michigan-Dearborn (Bachelor's in Business) and University of Detroit Mercy (Master's in Counseling). In middle school, I cried like a baby when I crossed the stage because I knew at that moment that there would be many moments in the future when I would miss thanking you. I want to also say thank you for choosing Mom to be your wife because she never missed a beat when you left. She worked to do her part every day to keep us close as a family, and I watched her sacrifice time and time again to make sure we had what we needed to live our lives. You picked a great woman, and a great mother for me.

So to wrap this letter up, I simply want to express my sincere and deepest gratitude to you for cultivating a young boy who grew up skinny, shy, reserved, and quiet, to one day become a man who realizes the value of each moment that I can make a difference. I have had good times and bad times, but through it all, I thank you for connecting me to my true Dad - My Heavenly Father. You told me to "look toward the hills from which cometh my help." You told me that He would never leave me neither forsake me. You told me that greater is He that is in me than he that is in the world. You told me that He is my wonderful counselor, my prince of peace, my strong hold, my everything, my grace from above, my light, my strength, my Shepard, and my comfort. I now know what you were preparing me for a life of destiny, and a life of purpose.

I want you to know that I thank you for all that you have done for me in my life. You would always say, "Son, what I am doing is not for me, but for you." Today I understand exactly what you meant, and your words continue to have meaning and purpose in my life.

I hope you know that I still love you, always will love you, and I thank God for your life.

With Love,
Adam

Dear God,

I am honored and extremely blessed to have had my Dad, who took the time to introduce me to you. When I think on your mercy and grace, I realize that you have blessed me to have the earthly parents involved in my upbringing to show me your goodness and magnificent power. As I look back on the life of my Dad and the role he played in my life, I am fortunate that he served as a role model and example of how to pray, how to worship, how to praise and how to serve you. I watched him serve as a beacon of hope for those who were less fortunate and a light in a dark place for a community that needed assistance. Back then, I didn't truly understand his commitment and purpose to serve you; but now that I am older, I understand his life's mission.

Father God, thank you for giving me the courage and strength to write this chapter and holding me through my pain and tears. I know that only you know how much I miss my Dad, and through your everlasting grace and mercy, you continue to give me the strength that I need each day. Some days the journey seems thick, tough and lonely; however, as long as I look up and keep my back straight, I know that you won't let anything ride me or wear me down.

Heavenly father, in this moment, let whoever reads these words realize the opportunity they have to turn to you as their father.

You are always a constant help in the time of need. Remind us of our value and the significant role that each of us plays in relationship to our families. Lord, bring estranged fathers back into the lives of their sons and daughters. Remind them of how important their role is and how a lack of their presence brings imbalance to the family structure and in the lives of their offspring. You are the one who can lift our heads in time of sorrow and give us strength in times of weakness. I look to you today because you are the everlasting father.

So on this very day, I believe that someone who reads this book and specifically this chapter will sign into the law of their heart a new Declaration of Dependence on you as their father for eternity. I believe that you will heal someone who has missed out on time spent with loved ones and sons and daughters. I believe you will bring new life to those who are physically alive and spiritually dead. I believe that you will give new vision, fresh ideas, and renewed dreams to your people. I say these words to you as I look to you.

Thank you for all that you've done, all that you are doing and all that you are going to do.

With love from a humble servant!

In Jesus Name,
Amen.

The Ultimate Goal

(Extended Version)
Originally Published in 2010
A Heart to Give: Journal of Transformation

If I can open my mouth
And let the truth be told,
If I can pray for the sick
Or inspire a soul,
If I can take what's broken
And with God's power make it whole,
Then I will be living within the expression
The true ultimate goal.

If I can serve my community
For as long as I live,
Showing empathy and compassion
And a heart to give,
Keeping my head held high
With faith, courage and strength to believe,

Then I know that God will be with me
And there will be nothing I cannot achieve.

The Vision is worth the dream.
Each step is worth the journey.
His purpose for my life is worth my destiny

About the Author

Since the time he could walk, Adam was involved in service with his family, helping local communities in Detroit, Michigan. After graduating from high school, Adam went on to attend the University of Michigan-Dearborn. Starting out as a student athlete and playing basketball his sophomore and junior years, Adam reunited with his core value and passion to be of service to local communities. Engaging in projects throughout Detroit during his senior year at University of Michigan, he began thinking about graduate school. He changed his major from business administration at University of Michigan to counseling for his Master's degree (University of Detroit Mercy). He really wanted to be of service to youth and young people because he realizes that they are the generation coming along.

Over the past few years, Adam has enjoyed coaching, mentoring and conducting workshops for youth and young adults on living their dreams. Adam has presented to schools, community organizations, conferences, colleges/universities, churches and in conversations that he has with the young people he mentors. Adam feels that every moment is an opportunity to make a difference, and that each person was born with unique talents and gifts to reveal to the world.

In the future, Adam hopes to do more traveling to learn about different cultures and ways of life. Adam plans to begin working on a third book as he considers doctorate programs. With a solid core group of family, colleagues and friends around him, Adam is grateful and thankful for the wealth of support people have poured into his life over the years. Adam plans to continue serving in the local community and being a part of the change that he hopes to see.

Made in the USA
Charleston, SC
01 October 2015